MINNESOTA
TWINS
STARS, STATS, HISTORY, AND MORE!

BY K. C. KELLEY

Published by The Child's World®
1980 Lookout Drive • Mankato, MN 56003-1705
800-599-READ • www.childsworld.com

ISBN 9781503828308
LCCN 2018944844

Printed in the United States of America
PAO2392

9/2019

Photo Credits:
Cover: Joe Robbins (2).
Interior: AP Images: 9, Mark Duncan 17, David Durochik
29; Dreamstime.com: Mark Herreid 13, Ron Hoff 20;
Newscom: Richard Tsong-Taatarii/Minneapolis
Star-Tribune/TNS 10, Mark Goldman/Icon SMI 19;
Joe Robbins 5, 6, 14, 23, 24, 27.

About the Author

K.C. Kelley is a huge sports
fan who has written more
than 100 books for kids. His
favorite sport is baseball.
He has also written about
football, basketball, soccer,
and even auto racing! He lives
in Santa Barbara, California.

On the Cover

Main photo: Star hitter
Eddie Rosario;
Inset: Twins hero Kirby Puckett

CONTENTS

GO, TWINS!

innesota Twins fans love their baseball team! The fans are loyal and loud! The team has given them a lot to cheer about over the years. The Twins had a long history before they came to Minnesota, too. Let's meet the Twins!

Max Kepler is one of the young Twins players ➤
hoping to bring home a trophy.

WHO ARE THE TWINS?

Minnesota plays in the American League (AL). That group is part of Major League Baseball (MLB). MLB also includes the National League (NL). There are 30 teams in MLB. The winner of the AL plays the winner of the NL in the **World Series**. The Twins won the World Series in 1987 and 1991. Their fans look forward to another title soon!

 *Joe Mauer won batting titles with the Twins in 2006, 2008, and 2009.*

WHERE THEY CAME FROM

The Minnesota Twins used to be the Washington Senators. That team started in the AL in 1901. The Senators played in Washington D.C. In 1961, the team move to Minnesota. It took the name Twins after Minneapolis and St. Paul. Together, that pair is known as the Twin Cities. The Twins have been a big part of their community ever since.

At the 1933 World Series, Senators manager Joe Cronin helps ➤
President Franklin Roosevelt throw out the first pitch.

WHO THEY PLAY

The Twins play in the AL Central Division. The other teams in the AL Central are the Chicago White Sox, the Cleveland Indians, the Detroit Tigers, and the Kansas City Royals. The Twins play more games against their division **rivals** than against other teams. In all, the Twins play 162 games each season. They play 81 games at home and 81 on the road. The Twins were in the AL West from 1969 to 1993.

◄ *Safe or out? Twins pitcher Lance Lynn was just ahead of Tigers baserunner Niko Goodrum. Out!*

WHERE THEY PLAY

For many years, the Twins played at the Metrodome. It was a huge indoor stadium. In 2010, the team moved to Target Field. This was much more like a traditional ballpark. It even had real grass, not **artificial turf**! Twins fans love their new home. Some call it the best place to watch a game in MLB!

The two guys shaking hands stand for the ➤
twin cities of Minneapolis and St. Paul.

THE BASEBALL FIELD

FOUL LINE

SECOND BASE ➤

THIRD BASE ▼

PITCHER'S MOUND

HOME PLATE

ON-DECK CIRCLE

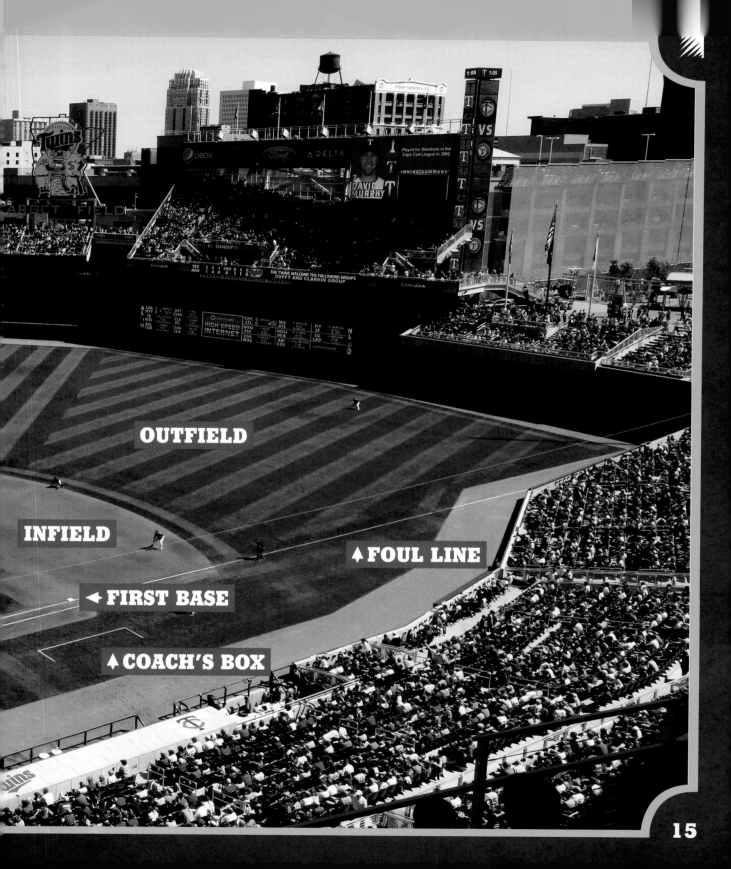

OUTFIELD

INFIELD

◄ FIRST BASE

▲ COACH'S BOX

▲ FOUL LINE

15

BIG DAYS

The Twins have had a lot of great days in their long history. Here are a few of them.

1924—This was the only World Series title in Senators history. Pitcher Walter Johnson led the team to a win over the New York Giants.

1987—The Twins won their first World Series in Minnesota. They beat the St. Louis Cardinals in seven games.

1991—This was one of the best World Series ever. The Twins won Game 7 1–0 in the tenth inning. They beat the Atlanta Braves.

Twins hero Kirby Puckett celebrates after ➤
leading his team to the 1991 championship.

TOUGH DAYS

ike every team, the Twins have had some not-so-great days, too. Here are a few their fans might not want to recall.

1904—The Senators had a lot of bad teams. This was the worst. They lost a team-record 113 games!

2002—The Twins **cut** a young player named David Ortiz. He went on to become a star with the Boston Red Sox. Ortiz hit 483 homers with Boston.

2006—Kirby Puckett was a much-loved Twins star. He had won the 1991 World Series MVP award. Sadly, he died this year at the age of 45.

Twins fans were sad every time David Ortiz ➤
smacked a homer after he left Minnesota.

MEET THE FANS!

Twins fans are famous for being loud! When the team played indoors, opponents sometimes could not even hear themselves! Since moving to Target Field, Twins fans stayed loyal. The team's **mascot**, T.C. Bear, helps fans cheer. His name stands for Twin Cities!

◄ *T.C. Bear is eager to help fans have a great time!*

HEROES THEN

ne of the best players in team history was on the Senators. Pitcher Walter "Big Train" Johnson is second all-time in MLB with 417 wins. Among Twins players, Rod Carew was probably the best hitter. He won seven AL batting titles. Harmon Killebrew was one of baseball's best **sluggers** in the 1960s. In the 1980s and 1990s, outfielder Kirby Puckett thrilled fans with his bat and his glove. First baseman Kent Hrbek smacked a lot of homers and helped the team win two World Series. Joe Mauer was one of the few catchers ever to lead the league in batting.

Puckett played every game full speed ahead! ➤

HEROES NOW

ddie Rosario is a homer-hitting young star. Miguel Sano is another big slugger for Minnesota. Behind the plate, Mitch Garver is a very good defensive catcher. Ehire Adrianza can play five positions! Pitcher Jose Berrios could be one of the best in the AL someday.

◄ *Look for Eddie Rosario to be a big star in the AL soon!*

GEARING UP

**B**aseball players wear team uniforms. On defense, they wear leather gloves to catch the ball. As batters, they wear hard helmets. This protects them from pitches. Batters hit the ball with long wood bats. Each player chooses his own size of bat. Catchers have the toughest job. They wear a lot of protection.

THE BASEBALL

The outside of the Major League baseball is made from cow leather. Two leather pieces shaped like 8s are stitched together. There are 108 stitches of red thread. These stitches help players grip the ball. Inside, the ball has a small center of cork and rubber. Hundreds of feet of yarn are tightly wound around this center.

CATCHER'S MASK AND HELMET

CHEST PROTECTOR

CATCHER'S MITT

WRIST BANDS

CATCHER'S GEAR

TEAM STATS

ere are some of the all-time career records for the Minnesota Twins. All these stats are through the 2018 regular season.

RBI

Harmon Killebrew	1,540
Kent Hrbek	1,086

STOLEN BASES

Clyde Milan	495
Sam Rice	346

BATTING AVERAGE

Rod Carew	.334
Henry Manush	.328

WINS

Walter Johnson	417
Jim Kaat	190

STRIKEOUTS

Walter Johnson	3,509
Bert Blyleven	2,035

SAVES

Joe Nathan	260
Rick Aguilera	254

Harmon Killebrew was one of the top sluggers of the 1960s. ➤

HOME RUNS

Harmon Killebrew	559
Kent Hrbek	293

GLOSSARY

artificial turf (art-uh-FISH-ul TURF) material made from plastic that takes the place of real grass

cut (KUT) in baseball, removing a player from a team's roster

mascot (MASS-kot) a costumed character who helps entertain fans

rivals (RYE-vuhlz) two people or groups competing for the same thing

sluggers (SLUG-erz) players who hit a lot of homers and extra-base hits

World Series (WURLD SEE-reez) the annual championship of Major League Baseball

FIND OUT MORE

IN THE LIBRARY

Connery-Boyd, Peg. *Minnesota Twins: Big Book of Activities*. Chicago, IL: Sourcebooks/Jabberwocky, 2016.

Gilbert, Sara. *World Series Champions: Minnesota Twins*. Mankato, MN: Creative Paperbacks, 2013.

Sports Illustrated Kids (editors). *Big Book of Who: Baseball*. New York, NY: Sports Illustrated Kids, 2017.

ON THE WEB

Visit our website for links about the Minnesota Twins:
childsworld.com/links

Note to Parents, Teachers, and Librarians: We routinely verify our web links to make sure they are safe and active sites. So encourage your readers to check them out!

INDEX